The Life and World of

ANNE FRANK

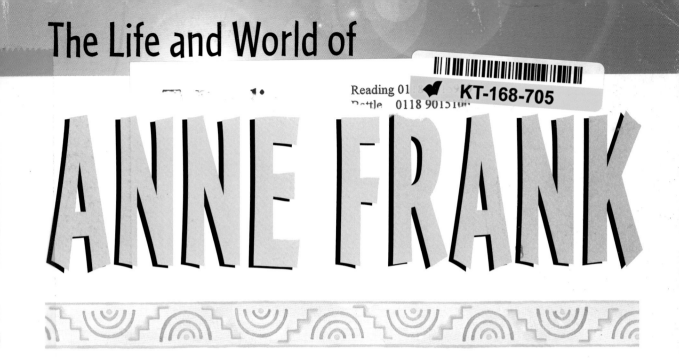

Brian Williams

Heinemann
LIBRARY

H www.heinemann/library.co.uk
Visit our website to find out more information about Heinemann Library books.

To order:
☎ Phone 44 (0) 1865 888066
▤ Send a fax to 44 (0) 1865 314091.
▭ Visit the Heinemann Library Bookshop at www.heinemann/library.co.uk to browse our catalogue and order online.

First published in Great Britain by Heinemann Library, Halley Court, Jordan Hill, Oxford OX2 8EJ, part of Harcourt Education.
Heinemann is a registered trademark of Harcourt Education Ltd.

Editorial: Lucy Thunder and Helen Cox
Design: Ron Kamen and Celia Floyd
Illustrations: Jeff Edwards and Joanna Brooker
Picture Research: Rebecca Sodergren and Elaine Willis
Production: Séverine Ribierre

Originated by Ambassador Litho Ltd
Printed and bound in China by W K T

ISBN 0 431 14780 9 (hardback)
07 06 05 04 03
10 9 8 7 6 5 4 3 2 1

ISBN 0 431 14787 6 (paperback)
08 07 06 05 04
10 9 8 7 6 5 4 3 2 1

British Library Cataloguing in Publication Data
Williams, Brian
Life and world of Anne Frank
940.5'318'092

A full catalogue record for this book is available from the British Library.

Acknowledgements
The publishers would like to thank the following for permission to reproduce photographs:
AKG pp. **10**, **11**, **12**, **14**, **18d**, **24**, **26**; Anne Frank House, The Netherlands pp. **19c**, **19e**, **22**, **29**; Corbis pp. **8**, **19a**, **28**; Hulton Archive pp. **4**, **6**, **9**, **18a**, **18b**, **18c**, **19b**, **19d**; Hulton Getty p. **7**; Imperial War Museum pp. **12**, **15**, **21**, **23**, **25**, **27**; Spaanestad Fotochief p. **20**; Topham Picturepoint p. **17**; Visual Image p. **16**.

Cover photograph of Anne Frank, reproduced with permission of Topham Picturepoint.

The publishers would like to thank Rebecca Vickers for her assistance in the preparation of this book.

Every effort has been made to contact copyright holders of any material reproduced in this book. Any omissions will be rectified in subsequent printings if notice is given to the publishers.

All quotes from Anne Frank's diary are copyright the Anne Frank Foundation.

Contents

Any words appearing in the text in bold, **like this**,
are explained in the Glossary.

Anne Frank remembered

Very few children stand out in history, but Anne Frank is an exception. She died when she was only fifteen. Yet Anne is remembered, because of what she wrote. She became a victim of the German **Nazis** during World War II (1939–45), when millions of **Jews** were killed in what became known as the **Holocaust**. However, Anne's diary was found by a friend and kept safe. After the war, it became a best-selling book, first in Dutch and later in 50 other languages. That diary tells us Anne Frank's story.

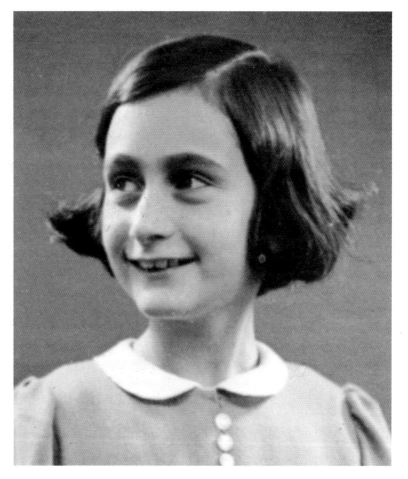

▲ Anne Frank was nine years old in this picture, taken the year before World War II began. She was enjoying her schooldays in the Dutch city of Amsterdam.

Europe at war

Anne was a German, but her family moved to the Netherlands in search of freedom. In Nazi Germany in the 1930s, Jews were victims of religious and race hatred. When war broke out in 1939, Jews all over Europe were in danger.

For over two years, Anne Frank and her family lived in hiding in a house in Amsterdam. In 1944 they were caught and sent to a **concentration camp**. When the war in Europe ended in May 1945 Anne was dead. So were her sister and mother. Only her father survived.

A dangerous adventure

'I want to see something of the world and do all kinds of exciting things,' Anne wrote on 8 May 1944. She was denied the chance. Yet, as she hoped, she lives on through her diary, written during what she called her 'dangerous adventure'. The diary has become a key piece of **evidence** for modern history. It shows us how one young girl faced the terrors of war and **persecution**. In her own words, Anne Frank grew into 'a woman with inward strength'.

▲ This map shows central Europe in 1939, the year World War II began. By 1941 only Britain and **neutral** Switzerland were free from Nazi control. The map also shows the concentration camps where Anne was held prisoner in 1944–45.

Key dates

1929	Anne Frank is born in Frankfurt, Germany
1934	Anne joins her family in Amsterdam
1939	World War II begins
1940	German armies invade the Netherlands
1942	(June) Anne is given a diary for her birthday
1942	(July) The Franks go into hiding
1944	The hiders are captured by the police
1945	Anne dies in March. World War II ends in August.
1960	The house in which Anne hid opens as a museum

Born in Germany

There had been Franks in Germany since the 1600s. Anne's father, Otto Frank, was born in 1889, in Frankfurt. He had met Anne's mother, Edith Holländer, while working in a bank. Like other Germans, Otto was trying to rebuild his life after fighting for the German Army during World War I (1914–18).

Hard times

Times were hard, for Germany had lost the war. It had to pay huge sums of money to the victors (Britain, France and the USA). Many Germans had no jobs, no money and no hopes. Otto and Edith married in 1925. A daughter, Margot, was born in 1926, and in 1929 the Franks had a second daughter, whom they named Annelies Marie. Everyone called her Anne. Anne was a bit of a scamp, always chattering and sometimes cheeky. Her father said there were two Annes: one good, one bad.

▲ Otto and Edith Frank were proud parents. Otto took many photographs of their growing children, Anne (right) and Margot (left).

The rise of the Nazis

When Anne was two, the family moved to a new home. It was smaller, but Anne liked the garden. The Franks moved to get away from their landlord, who was a member of the German **Nazi** party. The Nazis blamed **Jews** for Germany's troubles. Yet Mr Frank was proud of the medal he had won as a soldier. He was a Jew, but also a·German.

In 1933 the Nazi leader, Adolf Hitler, was elected to run the German government. Anti-Jewish **graffiti** began to appear on walls. Anne was looking forward to going to school in September 1933, but the Nazis brought in a new law to stop Jewish children from going to the same schools as non-Jews. Anne and Margot would have to find a new school.

◀ Frankfurt was (and still is) a busy city, famous as a banking centre. Many of the old buildings that the Franks knew, as pictured here in around 1925, were destroyed by bombs during World War II. Frankfurt was rebuilt after the war.

The Nazis

Adolf Hitler, a soldier who felt that Germans had been betrayed during World War I, led a small **political party**. In 1920, he changed its name to the National Socialist German Workers' Party. Members of the party became known as Nazis. Hitler and his Nazis ruled Germany from 1933. They preached anti-Semitism (hatred of Jews) and arrested anyone brave enough to speak out against Nazi ideas. They also prepared for a new war by building up the German army.

A new start

With Hitler in control, **Jews** no longer felt safe. In 1933, more than 60,000 German Jews left Germany. The Franks decided it was time to go, too. Anne's uncle Erich Elias ran a company making jam-making kits, and he suggested that Otto Frank start a branch of the firm in the Netherlands, a country close to Germany, but safer.

Moving to Amsterdam

Mr Frank found an apartment in Amsterdam and, in December 1933, Mrs Frank and Margot joined him there. Anne, not yet five, stayed in Germany to spend Christmas with her grandmother, before travelling to Amsterdam in time to celebrate Margot's eighth birthday.

Amsterdam was a city of canals, coffee shops and cyclists. Anne liked her new home at 37 Merwedeplein. She started school and soon spoke Dutch as well as German. Her teachers called her a chatterbox.

▼ Amsterdam is the biggest city in the Netherlands, and is famous for its canals. One canal, the Prinsengracht, was to be very important in Anne's life.

New friends

Among Anne's new friends were Lies Goosen and Sanne Houtman. They, too, were **refugees** from Germany. The girls made up a secret tune to whistle through one another's letterboxes, and swapped pictures of film stars. Anne loved going to the cinema. She also enjoyed swimming and skating, and was thrilled when the family went on a holiday visit to their relatives in Switzerland.

Anne liked to visit 'daddy's office'. There she met Miep Santrouschitz, her father's assistant, who showed her how to use a **typewriter**. She rode around Amsterdam on the **trams**, and learned to ride a bicycle. Many Dutch families went out for cycle rides at weekends. Life was happy and peaceful.

▲ **Anne at school in Amsterdam. She was popular, with lots of friends. Dutch schools, unlike German schools in the 1930s, welcomed children of all races and religions.**

Going to the cinema

Anne collected pictures of famous film stars. In the 1930s, many people went to the cinema at least once a week. There was no television, so going to the 'pictures' was very exciting. Cinema audiences watched news programmes, cartoons and Saturday serials, as well as films acted by famous film stars. In Germany, the **Nazis** used the cinema to spread their **propaganda**. Their films boasted of German greatness and put across their **racist** beliefs.

Fear grows

Anne had lived in Amsterdam for four years, when, in 1938, Mr Frank started a second business – selling herbs for the meat trade. His new partner, Mr van Pels, had a wife and a son, Peter, aged eleven. They had fled Germany in 1937, because they, too, were **Jews**.

Hitler makes more trouble

Hitler was never out of the news. He had sent German pilots and warplanes to fight in Spain (the civil war there was good practice for a bigger war). He had tried to make the 1936 Olympic Games in Germany a celebration of **Nazi** beliefs. By 1938 he had taken over neighbouring Austria. He also wanted to seize control of Czechoslovakia.

The Franks welcomed German Jewish **refugees** to their home for coffee and cakes on Saturday afternoons. Newcomers told how bad things were in Germany. Many Jews had fled to other countries. They were the lucky ones. Thousands of others had been arrested and sent to **concentration camps**. People lived in daily fear of the Gestapo, the German **secret police**.

◀ Passers-by look at the wreckage after 'Kristallnacht', 9–10 November 1938, when Nazi mobs attacked Jews and Jewish-owned shops. Many Jews decided after this that it was time to leave Germany, if they could.

Peace in our time

In Britain, people were already building bomb shelters in case of German **air raids**. Yet Neville Chamberlain, the British **prime minister**, said there would be no war. The Franks saw him on the cinema news. After talks with Adolf Hitler in September 1938, Chamberlain flew back to Britain, saying there would be 'peace in our time'.

Anne was not too worried about war. She was more interested in fun and games, school and sleepovers with her friends. She told her teacher she wanted to be a writer, or even a film star. She dreamed of visiting the USA – the land of peace, plenty and **Hollywood**.

In October 1938, the German army marched into Czechoslovakia. Hitler had won again. Few people now doubted that there would be war, soon.

▲ In April 1938, Germans and Austrians voted to unite in a new Nazi **empire**, or 'Reich'. Jews were not allowed to vote. This magazine cover shows crowds cheering Hitler in Vienna, Austria's capital city.

The Night of Breaking Glass

In November 1938, Mr Frank read the newspaper with a grim face. He told Margot and Anne about the dreadful events of 'Kristallnacht' (German for 'the night of breaking glass'). Throughout Germany, Nazi mobs had turned on Jews. In Berlin and other cities across the country, they had burned **synagogues** and smashed the windows of Jewish shops. Some Jews had even been beaten to death, while police stood by and did nothing.

It is war

On 1 September 1939, German troops and tanks smashed into Hitler's next target – Czechoslovakia's neighbour, Poland. Britain and France were **allies** of Poland, and on 3 September they declared war on Germany.

A new world war

Otto Frank remembered World War I (1914–18) only too clearly. What horrors would this new war bring? Anne and her family listened anxiously to the radio news. Poland was quickly overrun and, for Poland's many **Jews**, there was no escape. The Germans built new **concentration camps** there.

The winter of 1939–40 was icy cold. Anne and her friends went skating. Mr Frank moved his office to 263 Prinsengracht, an old red-brick house near the canal. Anne knew Mr Frank's staff – her Austrian friend Miep, and Miep's Dutch colleagues Bep Voskuijl, Johannes Kleiman and Victor Kugler. These four ran the office upstairs. On the ground floor, other workers mixed herbs and packed orders. Business went on, despite the war.

▲ Like other families, the Franks got war news from the radio. In the Netherlands, the Nazis took over radio stations, but people tuned in secretly to the **BBC**, or to Free Radio Orange, which was broadcast in Dutch from Britain.

The Netherlands invaded

The Germans had been waiting for spring. They overran Norway and Denmark. On Friday 10 May, Anne heard frightening news. The Germans had invaded the Netherlands and Belgium. In Amsterdam, people ran outside to see enemy planes overhead. Dutch radio warned everyone to stay indoors. On the same day, Winston Churchill took over from Neville Chamberlain as Britain's **prime minister**.

▲ German troops occupied the Netherlands in 1940. It was a shock to Anne to learn that some Dutch people welcomed the Nazis. Most hated the invaders and refused to help them in any way.

The small Dutch army could not stop German tanks and planes. On 14 May, the Dutch government surrendered. By 14 June, France, too, had fallen. Only Britain and its **empire** were still fighting the **Nazis**.

People on the move

Bombing was terrifying for Anne and her friends. In Britain, many children were being **evacuated** from the cities to the country, for fear of German **air raids**. Across the Netherlands, Belgium and France, many thousands of people had become **refugees**. Trying to escape from the Germans, they jammed the roads. Many refugees were Jews. By 1940, when the Nazis arrived, there were about 24,000 Jewish refugees in the Netherlands. Now there was no place else to go. There was to be no further escape from the Nazis.

Living under Nazi rule

The **Nazis** brought their hatred of **Jews** to the Netherlands. In October 1940, Anne learned that Mr Frank had to register his firm as a 'Jewish' business. Friends told of Jews being taken away in trucks. She saw signs reading 'No Jews' painted outside some restaurants and shops.

Life gets harder

The war news was bad. The British Royal Air Force had fought off German planes, to win the **Battle of Britain**. But across Europe, the Nazis ruled with an iron grip. From 1941, Dutch Jews had to have special **identity cards**, and could no longer take their money out of banks. All Jewish children had to go to Jewish schools. Anne and her Jewish friends were no longer allowed to play on public sports fields.

Trying to stay cheerful

They tried to stay cheerful. When the Germans invaded Russia in 1941, they told one another that Hitler had 'bitten off more than he could chew'. Anne's summer treat was Miep's wedding to Jan Gies in July 1941. She wore a new dress and showed off her new 'grown-up' hairstyle.

▲ Miep Santrouschitz married Jan Gies in July 1941.
Anne went to the wedding with her father.

In September 1941, at the age of twelve, Anne started her new school. She was glad that her best friend Lies was going, too. Anne enjoyed lessons, especially history and English. At home, when not playing table tennis, board games or gossiping about film stars, she read Greek myths. Anne loved these old tales of heroes defeating horrible monsters. She made up stories of her own, to amuse her friends and because she enjoyed writing.

▲ With so many men away fighting, women took over vital war work in industry. These women in a British factory are building aircraft for the Royal Air Force.

Women at war

The Nazis thought a woman's place was in the home. There were some women in the Nazi party, but all the top German Nazis were men. In Britain, women took jobs in factories, replacing men who were away fighting. Women also worked on farms, driving tractors and looking after the land. Others joined the women's branches of the armed forces.

Into hiding

In December 1941, the USA joined the war against the **Nazis**, after its naval base at Pearl Harbor was attacked by one of Germany's **allies** – Japan. The war was by now truly worldwide. American planes joined British bombers in **air raids** against enemy targets.

A worse time for Jews

1942 was an even worse year for Dutch **Jews**. They were banned from riding **trams** and owning bicycles. Anne was very sad, as she loved cycling. All Jews had to wear a yellow star on their clothes, and stay indoors from 8 p.m. until 6 a.m. Desperate to protect his family, Mr Frank talked to his friend Mr van Pels, and they decided it was time to 'disappear'.

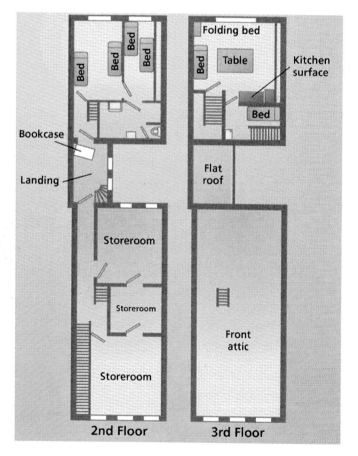

Thousands of Jewish families, unable to leave the Netherlands, had gone into hiding. Otto Frank planned to hide his family in the **annexe** behind the office. Miep Gies and the three other office workers willingly agreed to help.

Anne knew nothing of the plan. On 12 June, her thirteenth birthday, friends came to her party, to enjoy a film show. Among Anne's presents, 'possibly the nicest' was a diary. She pasted a photo of herself inside, and on Sunday 14 June she began writing.

▲ This is a plan of the secret annexe, where Anne and the others hid. Their rooms were on the second and third floors of 263 Prinsengracht, at the back of the office building.

The Franks disappear

On 8 July Anne wrote in her diary that the police had called with a letter. Margot had been ordered to get ready to go to a **work camp**. They might never see her again.

At once Mr Frank put his plan into action. Anne packed her things: diary, hair-curlers, hankies, combs and schoolbooks, but much had to be left behind. Everyone wore several layers of clothes. They left the house early in the morning, scribbling a hasty note for their **lodger**, Mr Goldschmidt. They walked four kilometres in pouring rain, entering the office before work had begun. Upstairs in the annexe, Anne looked around the bare rooms, with their blacked-out windows. This was to be home... for how long?

▶ Anne took her diary with her into hiding. These are pages from it. The picture pasted into the diary is Anne herself.

The Blitz

In 1940–41 German planes had begun bombing cities in Britain. This was the Blitz. **Air raids** were terrifying. People sat or slept in cellars or in bomb shelters while the bombs fell. Afterwards, lucky survivors cleared up the rubble and carried on as best they could. At night, there was a 'blackout', so that there were no lights on the ground to help the bombers see targets. Indoors, people covered windows with boards or thick curtains, to stop any lights showing.

Life in the annexe

A week after Anne and her family had 'disappeared', Mr and Mrs van Pels and Peter joined the Franks. Peter was now fifteen. He and Anne became friends, as the seven people settled down to a life in hiding.

Mr and Mrs Frank had one small room. Margot and Anne slept next door. They stuck postcards on the wall to cheer up the room. There was a tiny washroom and toilet. On the top floor was a room for the van Pels, with a table and cooker, and a cramped space for Peter.

Daily routine

In the secret **annexe**, the day began at 6.45 a.m. During the day, everyone had to move silently (in slippers) and speak softly. Only after 5.30 p.m., when the business closed, was it safe to peep out of a window or flush the toilet. At 9 p.m. everyone got ready for bed. It was hard to keep cheerful – 'after a while everything gets boring,' Anne later wrote in her diary.

 ▲ Otto Frank

 ▲ Edith Frank

 ▲ Margot Frank

 ▲ Anne Frank

Tuning in to London

People in countries captured by the **Nazis** listened in secret to radio broadcasts from the BBC in London for news of the war. Often people in Britain sent **code messages** by radio to friends in occupied countries. Some messages were secret signals to people in the **Resistance**, the 'underground armies' resisting the Nazi invaders.

Passing the time

At night, the hiders crept downstairs to listen to the office radio. The **BBC** spoke of Nazi 'death-camps' in which **Jews** were killed in gas-filled rooms. It seemed too awful to be true.

Mr Frank gave the three teenagers lessons in maths, geography, history and languages. Anne did her writing in the attic at the top of the house. The diary now had a name. 'Dear Kitty', she wrote on 10 July 1942, after describing her new home 'I expect I have thoroughly bored you... but still I think you should know where we've landed.'

▲ The door to the secret annexe. A hinged bookcase hid the entrance, making the people inside feel a little bit safer.

Anne's secret names

Anne invented secret names to use in the diary, to disguise the real names of her friends.

Real name	Diary name
Johannes Kleiman	Mr Koophuis
Victor Kugler	Mr Kraler
Bep Voskuijl	Elli Vossen
Miep Gies	Miep van Santen
Jan Gies	Henk van Santen
The van Pels family	The van Daans
Fritz Pfeffer (the 8th and last hider)	Albert Dussel

▲ Mr van Pels

▲ Mrs van Pels

▲ Peter van Pels

▲ Fritz Pfeffer

Celebrations and fears

In November 1942, the seven hiders became eight. Fritz Pfeffer, Miep's dentist, joined Anne and the others. Not even his wife knew where he had gone. Mr Pfeffer shared the girls' room. The **annexe** was now rather crowded, and there were arguments. Anne got rid of her cross feelings by writing in her diary.

Food and little feasts

'Our helpers display heroism in their cheerfulness and affection,' Anne wrote. Miep and the others never forgot them. A friendly baker brought bread to the office, and a greengrocer left potatoes, which were hidden in a cupboard. After dark, Peter would go downstairs to collect the potatoes.

The hiders celebrated special days: Christmas, the Jewish festival of Hanukkah and St Nicholas' Eve on 5 December, the day when Dutch people exchange gifts. They lit candles and made small presents, which Anne and Miep hid in shoes inside a basket.

◄ This is Anne's special Christmas diary page for 27 December 1943. She wrote neatly, in Dutch, and stuck in cut-out pictures from cards and magazines. When the diary was full, she wrote in office notebooks.

Scares and alarms

Time passed very slowly. When Miep came to visit, Anne jumped up eagerly to ask for news. She so missed fresh air. 'When someone comes in from outside, with the wind in their clothes and the cold air on their faces, then I could bury my head in the blankets,' she wrote in December 1943. The news was still bad. Miep said that **Jews** were still being arrested. Some wandered the streets all day, hoping to escape the police at their door.

By 1944, after a second winter in hiding, everyone looked pale and thin. Luckily no one had been seriously ill. There was never enough to eat, yet Anne had outgrown her clothes. She was delighted when Miep brought her a pair of second-hand high-heeled shoes, bright red.

Burglars broke into the building three times. The last time, in April 1944, was the most frightening. The thieves were scared off, but then after the weekend the police came and poked around downstairs to investigate. 'Eight hearts pounded,' wrote Anne. They were so terrified of being discovered.

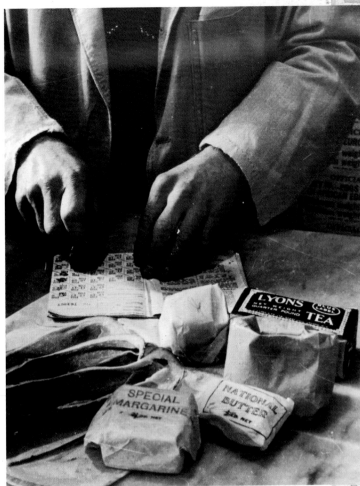

▲ People in Britain, like the Dutch, had ration books. Anne's helpers used forged (fake) **ration coupons**. Without them, they could not buy food for the hiders.

Food rationing

A typical menu for Anne and her family was: dry bread or porridge (bread and jam was a real treat!) for breakfast; spinach or lettuce for lunch; fried potatoes for tea. In Britain, too, many people were used to going hungry. Many foods were rationed to make sure everyone got a fair share. People got used to going without luxuries, such as sugar, bananas and sweets.

Hopes rise

The spring of 1944 brought new hopes. The **Allies** seemed to be winning in Italy and in Russia. Mr Frank and Anne cheerfully told the others the war would soon be over. Watching a chestnut tree outside burst into leaf, Anne wondered if she would be back in school by the time the leaves turned brown in autumn.

Anne and Peter, who was now seventeen, spent more time together. Anne wrote about her feelings for him. It felt nice to be 'in love', but was it 'scandalous' to feel like this when she was not yet fifteen?

Writing for others to read

In March, the Dutch government asked people in a radio message to keep war diaries and letters, for future generations to read. Anne wanted to become Dutch after the war, to write books and so 'go on living even after my death'. She began revising the many pages of diary she had written since 1942.

'Friends are on the way'

The most exciting day was D-Day, 6 June 1944. Everyone listened to the radio, cheering the news that Allied armies had landed in France. Mr Frank stuck pins on a map to show how the Germans were being pushed back. 'Will this year, 1944, bring us victory? We don't know yet. But where there's hope, there's life. It fills us with fresh courage and makes us strong again,' Anne wrote in her diary for 6 June.

▲ This is the Westerkerk church clock. Anne could see it from the front attic window. It chimed every 15 minutes. How long each day must have seemed.

Summer treats

On 12 June 1944, Anne was fifteen and there were birthday presents from everyone. Peter gave her flowers (brought by Miep), her parents gave her a book, Margot gave her a bracelet. Anne was looking forward to the future. 'My start has been so very full of interest,' she wrote. 'I still believe that people are really good at heart.'

▲ On D-Day, a huge fleet carried the **Allies** across the Channel from England to Normandy, in France. This was the biggest invasion by sea in history, yet it took another year of fighting before the war ended.

D-Day, 6 June 1944

D-Day was the **code name** for the Allies' invasion of France in June 1944. An army of many nations landed by sea and air, to begin the fight to free Europe from the grip of the **Nazis**. Anne wrote in her diary: 'Oh Kitty, the best part about the invasion is that I have the feeling that friends are on the way.'

Arrest

On 1 August 1944 Anne wrote her diary as usual. She was writing about growing up and learning to keep silent, even when angry. 'I never utter my real feelings about anything,' she wrote, calling herself 'a little bundle of contradictions'. This was to be her last entry.

The day begins quietly

On 4 August, Miep came to collect the shopping list, promising to stay for a proper chat with Anne after lunch. Mr Frank began giving Peter an English lesson.

In the office, Miep and the others got on with their work. Suddenly, a car drew up. The door opened and five policemen came in. One was Austrian; Miep recognized his accent. The police said they knew **Jews** were hiding in the building. The bookcase was pulled back, and they went upstairs.

The hiders are captured

It must have been a terrifying moment when the police burst in, shouting angrily. The Austrian policeman, Karl Silberbauer, looked surprised when Mr Frank told him he had fought in the German army during World War I. It made no difference. The police took money and jewellery, then Miep heard the sound of 'our friends' feet' coming down the stairs.

◄ Jews on their way to captivity. Anne and her family were sent to Westerbork, a Dutch **concentration camp**. The Franks' names appear on a Nazi list of prisoners there, dated 3 September 1944.

From across the canal, Jan Gies watched the eight taken away in a truck. Mr Kleiman and Mr Kugler were arrested, too. After the police had gone, Miep went upstairs. The rooms were in a mess. Miep picked up the family photo album, Anne's diary books and the shawl Anne wore when combing her hair. Next day, Miep bravely went to police headquarters to seek her friends' release. The police sometimes took **bribes**. This time it was no use.

▲ Joyful crowds welcomed the **Allies** into Paris on 26 August 1944. France was free, but Anne and her friends were captives.

Resisters and betrayers

The hiders had been betrayed, or possibly seen by people in a nearby house. It is not known who told the police about the secret **annexe**. Some Dutch people helped the **Nazis**, as **collaborators**. Others, like Jan Gies, joined the **Resistance**. Although brave helpers like Miep and Jan saved 16,000 Jews hiding in the Netherlands, 9000 other Jews, like Anne, were captured. Many Dutch freedom-fighters were executed by the Nazis – fighting back was very dangerous.

Death camps

In Westerbork camp, Anne had her head shaved like the other prisoners. Everyone had to work, taking used batteries to pieces. On 3 September, the eight friends (still together) were put on a train. Crushed into a goods wagon with 70 other prisoners, they were taken east for three days, to Auschwitz in Poland.

The family is separated

At Auschwitz, men and women were split up. Anne, Margot and Mrs Frank were taken to the nearby women's camp at Birkenau. Anne never saw her father again. Auschwitz was a death camp. Old people, sick people and children younger than fifteen were killed by poison gas soon after they arrived. The rest were forced to work until they died of hunger, sickness or despair.

Death in the camps

Mr van Pels died in a gas chamber at Auschwitz. In October 1944, Anne, Margot and Mrs van Pels were taken from Birkenau to Bergen-Belsen camp in Germany. Mrs Frank was left behind, very weak, and she died in January 1945. Mr Pfeffer was moved to a camp in Germany, where he died in December 1944. Mrs van Pels was also moved on, and she died in a camp in Czechoslovakia in the spring of 1945. Peter died in an Austrian prison camp called Mauthausen.

▶ **During the last winter of the war, 1944–45, 20,000 Dutch people died of hunger and cold. Allied planes dropped food supplies, as well as soldiers, by parachute as they fought to free the Netherlands.**

Anne's last days

Anne and Margot spent a terrible winter in Bergen-Belsen camp. Margot became very ill, with **typhus**, and died during February or March 1945. Anne's schoolfriend Lies was also a prisoner in Belsen, and saw Anne through the wire fence. Two friends from Westerbork, Janny and Lientje Brilleslijper, remembered how Anne told stories, even as she sickened with typhus and exhaustion. Towards the end of March, she died. No one knows exactly when she gave up.

On 15 April 1945, British soldiers drove into Bergen-Belsen, and rescued those who were still alive. Lies, Janny and Lientje were among the survivors. Otto Frank, too, was still alive.

▲ When the British entered Bergen-Belsen, they were sickened by what they saw. They found mass graves, full of dead bodies. The survivors looked like living skeletons. Here, British soldiers are giving out food to inmates of the camp.

The Holocaust

Persecution of **Jews** (anti-Semitism) has caused much suffering for hundreds of years. The **Nazi** leader, Adolf Hitler, hated Jews. The Nazis forced Jews to live in special areas called **ghettos**, and to work as slaves. From 1941, the Nazis began to murder Jews in special camps, by gassing them. Camps became 'factories of death'. This was the **Holocaust**. At least six million Jews and other people captured by the Nazis were murdered in this way, or died of injuries, starvation or disease.

Anne's legacy

The Dutch had to wait until May 1945 for freedom. During the last cruel winter of war, cold and hungry, Miep and the others longed for news of their friends. As British and American troops found more **Nazi** death camps, the full horrors of the **Holocaust** came to light.

A surprise homecoming

On 3 June 1945, Otto Frank came home. He had been freed from Auschwitz by the Russians in January 1945. Miep told him her good news: Mr Kleiman and Mr Kugler were both safe. What of Anne, Margot, Mrs Frank and the others?

Mr Frank said he knew his wife was dead. He knew nothing of Anne or Margot. Lists of prisoners' names were being checked, so he still hoped. In July 1945, Mr Frank learned the terrible news. Anne and Margot were dead.

The diary reaches the world

Miep Gies handed Anne's diary to Mr Frank. 'Here is your daughter's legacy to you,' she told him. He sat down to read. Mr Frank copied out the diary for his mother and sister.

▲ Anne's diary has been translated into 50 languages. Scientific tests have proved that the diary is genuine. Some doubters said it could not have been written by a person as young as Anne.

Later, at a friend's suggestion, he let Anne's book be published. The diary was printed in Dutch as *Het Achterhuis* (*The Annexe*) in 1947. The first English version was in 1951. Anne's story was made into a stage play in 1956 and filmed in 1959. In 1960 the house at 263 Prinsengracht became a museum.

In 1953, Otto Frank moved to Switzerland. He married again; his wife, too, was an Auschwitz survivor. He died in 1980, aged 91.

Anne Frank's memory lives

'Will I ever be able to write anything great?' Anne wrote in April 1944. She had, and she did indeed 'live on' through her writing, as she wished. Her diary became a memorial to the millions like her who died in the **Holocaust**. The Anne Frank Foundation and the Anne Frank Trust work to educate young people about the dangers of **racism** and intolerance. Anne's life became a symbol of hope, the hope that never again shall such evil cause so much suffering.

▶ This is the house at 263 Prinsengracht in Amsterdam, as it looks today. 'Just imagine,' Anne wrote on 29 March 1944, 'how interesting it would be if I were to publish a novel about the Secret Annexe. The title alone would make people think it was a detective story.' Over 30 million copies of her diary have been sold.

Glossary

air raid   attack by aircraft dropping bombs on cities and military targets

allies   partners in a fight against an enemy; the Allies in World War II were the countries fighting Germany, Italy and Japan

annexe   extra rooms built on to a house

Battle of Britain   air battle between the Royal Air Force and the German Air Force or *Luftwaffe* in 1940

BBC   short for British Broadcasting Corporation

bribe   payment offered in return for a favour

code name   secret name for a secret mission in wartime

code messages   writing or other messages sent in a disguised form

collaborators   people who help an enemy invader of their country

concentration camp   camp for holding political prisoners, sent there without trial

empire   several countries, all ruled by one person or government. The British Empire became the Commonwealth.

evacuated   taken to a safe place

evidence   what is learned about history from writings, old objects and people's memories

ghetto   sealed area of a town in which Jews were forced to live

graffiti   writing on walls

Hollywood   place in California, home of the USA's film industry

Holocaust   Nazi mass murder of Jews and other groups during World War II

identity card   paper with someone's name, photo and personal details

Jews   followers of the religion of Judaism

lodger   someone who pays for a room in another person's home

Nazi   member of the German National Socialist Workers Party

neutral   taking neither side in a war

persecution   deliberate cruel treatment

political party   group of people with the same ideas about how a country should be governed

prime minister   the name of the leader of the government in Britain and in many other countries

propaganda   spreading ideas, usually false ideas

racism   belief that one race is superior to another, and treating people of another race unfairly

ration coupons   special permits to buy rationed goods, such as food or clothes, during World War II

refugees   people forced to leave their homes because of natural disaster, famine, persecution or war

Resistance   fighting back against an enemy; the Dutch resisted the German invaders of their country

secret police   special police used to hunt down opponents of a government

synagogue   Jewish place of religious worship

trams   public transport system using electric cars on rails

typhus   dangerous disease spread by dirt and body lice

typewriter   office machine used for writing letters

work camp   prison to which the Nazis sent people to work as slaves

Timeline

1918   World War I ends with Germany's defeat

1929   Anne Frank is born in Frankfurt

1933   Adolf Hitler becomes leader of Germany. The Franks move to the Netherlands.

1938   Persecution of Jews in Germany worsens

1939   World War II begins

1940   The Netherlands are invaded. German armies control most of Europe.

1941   The Germans invade Russia. The Japanese attack the US base at Pearl Harbor, Hawaii.

1942   Anne Frank goes into hiding. She begins her diary.

1944   In June, the Allies invade France. In August, the Frank family and their friends are caught by the police.

1945   Anne Frank dies in Bergen-Belsen concentration camp (March). Hitler kills himself (April). The war in Europe ends on 4 May.

1947   Anne Frank's diary is first published, in Dutch

Further reading & websites

Anne Frank Remembered, Miep Gies and Alison Leslie Gold (Bantam, 1987)

Anne Frank's Story, Carol Anne Lee (Puffin Books, 2001)

Profiles: Anne Frank, Richard Tames (Heinemann Library, 1998)

The Diary of Anne Frank, various editions since first British edition, 1952

Heinemann Explore – an online resource from Heinemann.
For Key Stage 2 history go to *www.heinemannexplore.co.uk*

http://www.afet.org.uk – website of the Anne Frank Educational Trust

http://www.annefrank.ch/ – website of the Anne Frank Foundation

Places to visit

Imperial War Museum, London and Manchester

Anne Frank Museum, 263 Prinsengracht, Amsterdam, the Netherlands

Index